False Pretences

A comedy

Eric Chappell

Samuel French — London
www.samuelfrench-london.co.uk

FOR AMATEUR PRODUCTION ENQUIRIES

UNITED KINGDOM AND WORLD EXCLUDING NORTH AMERICA

plays@SamuelFrench-London.co.uk

020 7255 4302/01

Each title is subject to availability from Samuel French,

depending upon country of performance.

CHARACTERS

Kevin, an estate agent; late 30s
Valerie, his wife; 30s
Lucy, their vivacious friend; 30s
Victor, Valerie's brother; early 40s
Tank Turner, the bank manager; 50
Soapy Simpson, 30s
Toby, a jeweller; 40s

COPYRIGHT INFORMATION

(See also page ii)

The play was derived from the author's television series *The Bounder*, starring Peter Bowles and George Cole.

Other plays by Eric Chappell
published by Samuel French Ltd

Cut and Dried (from *Fiddlers Three*)
Double Vision
Father's Day
Fiddlers Three (comprising Cut and Dried
and We Don't Want to Lose you)
Haunted
Haywire
Heatstroke
It Can Damage Your Health
Natural Causes
Something's Burning
Summer End
Theft
Up and Coming
We Don't Want to Lose You (from *Fiddlers Three*)
Wife After Death

ACT I

SCENE 1

Kevin and Valerie Bunce's living-room. Early evening

*A spacious room with reproduction furniture and a chintz-covered suite.
A simulated log effect fire glows in the Regency-style fireplace. Upstage
stands a leather-topped desk with phone and high-backed swivel chair.* L
*of the desk are french doors, usually open, which lead into a long, glass
conservatory, with ferns and flowers, which continues out of sight* L. *A
window,* DR, *gives a partial view of the road. Beyond the conservatory
is a broad, suburban garden. A revolving cocktail cabinet stands* DL. *A
door,* R, *leads off to the hall. The effect of the room is of someone aiming
for good taste and missing slightly*

As the CURTAIN *rises, Kevin Bunce enters from the hall, carrying a briefcase. He is a soberly dressed man in his late thirties. He is given to deep
internal groaning when things go wrong which he accomplishes without
moving his lips, but at the moment he is wearing a self-satisfied smile*

Kevin (*throwing down his briefcase*) Val, where are you?

*Valerie Bunce follows him almost at once. She is a few years younger
than her husband with a warm smile faintly tinged at the moment with
apprehension*

Kevin turns

Has she arrived?
Valerie Yes … (*She glances anxiously back towards the hall*)
Kevin Is something wrong?
Valerie No.
Kevin She's all right? She's not still grieving?
Valerie No — it has been a couple of years. She's over all that. Life
moves on.
Kevin That's true. It would be nice if she met someone.
Valerie (*another look back*) Yes …

He regards her uncertainly

(*Brightly*) Had a good day?

Kevin Yes. I think I've finally sold Greenacres.

Valerie The house by the crematorium?

Kevin (*frowning*) I didn't mention that.

Valerie Oh.

Kevin I thought you'd be pleased.

Valerie I am. This calls for a drink. (*She crosses to the cabinet and begins to pour*)

Kevin Well, it is a little early but why not? It'll be nice seeing Lucy again. I don't think we've met since her wedding … (*He takes a drink and chokes*) God! This is strong.

Valerie I thought you liked it strong.

Kevin Yes, but not lethal. (*Suspiciously*) There is something wrong, isn't there?

Valerie closes the door and hesitates

Valerie Yes.

Kevin Is it your brother?

Valerie (*sitting*) It's been a bit of a shock …

Kevin (*hopefully*) Is he … dead?

Valerie No, he's out.

Kevin Well, he's not coming here.

Valerie He is here.

Kevin Then get rid of him.

Valerie I can't. He's my brother — and your best man. And he's very fond of us.

Kevin If he's fond of us why doesn't he stay away? (*Concerned*) Has Lucy met him?

Valerie No, she was changing for dinner.

Kevin Good. Get him out of the house before she comes down.

Valerie I can't ask him to leave. We haven't seen him in years.

Kevin Of course we haven't. (*Hissing*) He's been in prison. If we'd wanted him to call we'd have had to send him a cake with a file in it!

Valerie checks that the hall door is firmly closed

Valerie I hope you won't keep mentioning that.

Kevin What?

Valerie That he's been in prison.

Kevin Don't worry. I shan't mention it at all. I'm trying to keep it quiet. I have my reputation to think of.

Valerie I wasn't thinking of your reputation — I was thinking of his. He has paid his debt to society, Kevin.

Kevin He may have paid his debt to society but he still owes me a few quid. (*Pointing to a vase on the mantelpiece*) He hasn't paid for his wedding present yet — and that was ten years ago! He still owes us for that vase.

Valerie Kevin, you're getting agitated. You know it's bad for your digestion.

Kevin And what about Rockfast Investments Ltd? They may not have been fast but my God, they were certainly rocky!

Valerie That wasn't his fault. He never was good at figures.

Kevin He certainly wasn't.

Valerie He did nothing wrong. He was innocent. I'm not ashamed of my brother.

Kevin Aren't you? Then why do you never mention him?

Valerie I do.

Kevin Have you mentioned him to Lucy?

Valerie Well, no ...

Kevin Does she even know he exists?

Valerie I've no idea.

Kevin It seems I'm not the only one who's ashamed of him.

Valerie (*after a pause*) He's changed.

Kevin He hasn't changed. (*Sitting*) He'll still patronize me. It may be years but he'll come in here as if it were only yesterday — and my collar will start to prickle. He'll take my chair. He'll take my desk. And he'll call me Kev. If he calls me Kev — I swear I'll go for him.

Valerie Perhaps you'll feel differently when you see him.

Kevin What do you mean?

Valerie Prison's left its mark I'm afraid. You'll be surprised at the change in him. So try and act naturally.

Kevin Don't worry, I intend to act naturally. I've only one thing to say to your brother and that's —— (*He breaks off*)

Victor Blake enters the room. Victor is pale, well groomed, and leaning heavily on a stick. He is in his early forties. He gives Kevin a brave smile

Victor Hello, Kev.
Kevin (*staring*) Victor.

Victor limps forward to take Kevin's hand

Victor It's been a long time.
Kevin (*rising*) Yes.
Victor Thank you. (*He takes Kevin's chair and looks around*) Nice to be back in the old room. Is that a real fire, Kev?

Kevin (*suspiciously*) No — it's a simulated log effect.

Victor A simulated log effect! Well, you could have fooled me. What will they think of next? Ah! (*Pointing at the vase with his stick*) You still have it. "Thou unravished bride of quietness."

Kevin What?

Victor The vase. Look after it. I won't tell you how much it cost.

Kevin (*bleakly*) We know.

Valerie (*quickly*) We do love it, Victor.

Kevin Drink, Victor?

Victor Thanks. A scotch.

Kevin proudly spins the cocktail cabinet towards him

Hm. I didn't know they still made those …

Kevin frowns and hands Victor his drink

Kevin Er, will you be staying long, Victor?

Victor Now, Kev — don't start that. Don't press me to stay because I can't. I must find a place of my own.

Kevin (*relieved*) Of course.

Victor I can only stay a few weeks.

Kevin Weeks?

Victor Sorry, Kev — I can't make it any longer.

Kevin You mean just until you get on your feet …

Silence. Victor looks down at his leg and sighs

Victor You could say that …

Valerie (*frowning*) Kevin meant until you find a place of your own.

Victor Yes, you could be useful there, Kev.

Kevin You mean a place around here?

Valerie Of course he means a place around here. I'm sure Kevin can find something, Victor.

Victor Good. The sooner the better. After all, two's company — three's a crowd.

Kevin But it's not three — it's four.

Victor Four?

Kevin Yes.

Victor looks from one to the other

Victor Congratulations! I didn't know. This calls for a big cigar, Kevin. I'm delighted. To tell the truth, I always thought there was something wrong …

Kevin (*sharply*) I'm not a father, Victor. We have a guest.
Valerie An old school friend.
Kevin (*with emphasis*) A widow. Recently bereaved. Been through a great deal. Picking up the pieces. Not strong. Needs peace and quiet.

Victor regards them thoughtfully

Victor And you think I'll be in the way.
Valerie No.
Victor Does she know I'm here?

Kevin and Valerie exchange glances

Valerie Er, no.
Victor You haven't told her?
Valerie Not yet.
Victor So if I were to tiptoe out of here, she'd never know.
Valerie There's no need for that, Victor.
Victor I think there's every need. I can understand your embarrassment — and if I could tiptoe, I would, unfortunately I can't. (*He looks broodingly at his stick. He rises awkwardly*) Could you bring my case down, Kevin. The stairs are a problem.
Kevin Certainly.
Valerie No, Kevin. Victor, at least stay for dinner.
Kevin (*glumly*) Dinner?
Victor (*sitting*) You're very sweet, Val but I'd hate to embarrass you.
Valerie You've never embarrassed me, Victor. (*A sharp glance at Kevin*) I'll start dinner — and I'll tell Lucy you're here — and you can stay as long as you like.

An internal groan from Kevin

Valerie exits

Victor Lucy. Delightful name.
Kevin Yes.

Kevin watches Victor as he rises from his chair, his face contorted in pain, and limps across the room. Kevin hastily takes possession of his chair then realizes that Victor has taken possession of his desk

Victor Is this the sort of desk that comes apart?
Kevin (*frowning*) Yes.

Victor I thought it was that sort of desk. Must be careful. Don't want it to come to pieces ... (*He swings round in the chair*) Nice view of the garden. Hope I shall be able to concentrate on my work.

Kevin What work? You haven't got any work.

Victor I have been prepared for life outside, Kevin. It wasn't all sewing mailbags. We had courses for everything. Pottery, Bricklaying, Art classes.

Kevin What did you choose? Creative writing?

Victor How did you guess?

Kevin It's the obvious choice. You certainly showed plenty of creativity when you prepared the prospectus for Rockfast Investments. Why not write your life story. You could call it "A Fair Cop".

Victor (*sighing*) I hope it isn't always going to be like this, Kev. The prejudice — the distrust.

Kevin Victor, we have a good life here. I have friends, I've become respected and trusted. And that's not easy for an estate agent.

Victor I see. What do you tell your friends about me?

Kevin I say you went abroad.

Victor Abroad.

Kevin The Congo.

Victor The Congo! Kevin, are you ashamed of me?

Kevin Yes.

Victor Let me tell you something, Kevin, there were four hundred men in that hellhole.

Kevin Hellhole! It was an open prison!

Victor Four hundred pretty tough characters — ruthless and hard-bitten. They'd seen it all — you couldn't fool them. They all said there were only two men in that place who were innocent — myself and the governor. Although I wasn't entirely sure about the governor.

Kevin How can you say that? The evidence was overwhelming. You haven't a leg to stand on ... (*He breaks off*)

They regard Victor's leg

Victor (*sighing*) That's true.

Kevin Sorry, Victor, I didn't mean ...

Victor I took most of the blame to protect my accountant. He had a wife and six children. I haven't seen him since and neither have they. My mistake was that I believed in people. (*Emotionally*) But do I have to pay for that mistake for the rest of my life?

Kevin Of course not.

Victor All I ask is a chance to bury the past.

Kevin I'll get a spade.

Victor (*smiling*) Good man. We'll strike a bargain. You won't tell your friends I've been in prison — I won't tell mine you're an estate agent.
Kevin What!

Valerie and Lucy enter. Lucy is nothing like Kevin's description. She is an attractive, vivacious woman in her thirties with a mischievous smile

Lucy ...

He embraces her

Lucy Kevin.
Valerie Lucy, this is my brother, Victor. Victor — Lucy.
Victor (*holding out a tired hand*) Forgive me for not rising only my doctors have advised me not to stand ...
Lucy I do understand. Val told me. I must say, until now, I didn't know you had a brother, Val.
Kevin (*hastily*) Let me get you a drink, Lucy. Sherry? Gin and tonic? (*He whirls the cocktail cabinet around*)
Valerie He's been away — it's been years.
Lucy But you've never mentioned him once.

Valerie becomes flustered by Victor's stern gaze

Valerie It was too painful.
Lucy Why?
Kevin Dry white wine?
Valerie We didn't know when he'd come out.
Kevin Scotch!
Lucy Out? Out of where?

Valerie and Kevin look desperate

Valerie Hospital.
Kevin The jungle.
Lucy (*staring*) A hospital in the jungle.

An internal groan from Kevin that he turns into a cough

Victor (*smoothly*) Val, you could hardly call that place a hospital. Just a few primitive dwellings and a missionary. (*To Lucy*) They took me there after I was gored.

Lucy Gored!

Victor Charging rhino. Rifle jammed. Tried staring it out but the porters panicked. They carried me for days on a simple litter — rambling and incoherent — then one morning I felt this cool hand on my brow. I found myself gazing into the eyes of a beautiful nun. For a moment I thought I was in heaven.

Kevin (*desperately*) Gin and It? Gin and orange? Gin and lime?

Lucy I must say I find that hard to believe.

Victor What?

Lucy That you were ever rambling and incoherent.

Victor I know it's hard to believe now, Lucy, sitting here in this comfortable suburban drawing-room — or do you call it a lounge, Kev?

Kevin (*frowning*) No.

Victor In this comfortable suburban drawing-room with a simulated log effect burning in the grate ... It seems light years away.

Lucy Were you out there long?

Victor I stayed on after I recovered. I felt I had to give something back. Worked amongst the lepers for some years.

Lucy Lepers?

Another muted groan from Kevin

Victor But circumstances forced me to leave.

Lucy Not leprosy as well?

Victor No. The nun and I had become rather too close to each other. She had begun to leave off her rosary, which was rather worrying. I thought it was time to move on.

Valerie (*suddenly*) I think I'd better get dinner.

Victor Ah. I promised my doctors I'd take a short stroll before dinner. Perhaps just round the rose garden ... (*He rises with difficulty*) Lucy, could I borrow your shoulder?

Lucy Certainly ...

Lucy assists Victor through the conservatory into the garden

Kevin (*groaning*) Oh, no!

Valerie What's the matter?

Kevin My collar's started to prickle. Did you hear all that? She didn't believe a word of it.

Valerie He can be very persuasive. He once persuaded his young cousins they were fairies and they flew straight out of the bedroom window.

Kevin She was laughing at him.

Valerie Well, she hasn't had much to laugh about these last few years.

Kevin Gored by a rhino! And what about the leper colony?

Valerie Well, you introduced the jungle. The trouble is he gets carried away.

Kevin (*bitterly*) I wish he would — on a litter — rambling and incoherent. And did you hear that snide remark about our simulated log effect?

Valerie Kevin, he's staying — at least until he's better.

Kevin I suppose he does need that stick?

Valerie Of course he does. Why do you say that?

Kevin He seems to be flourishing it a great deal — almost as if he's just got it. Probably took it from a cripple.

Valerie crosses and looks out into the garden

Valerie You can see he's not well.

Kevin joins her

Kevin What about that limp? First it's one leg then the other — he doesn't seem to be able to make up his mind.

Valerie That's your imagination. (*Pause*) They look good together, don't they?

Kevin What?

Valerie They make an attractive couple.

Kevin Don't start that.

Valerie What?

Kevin Matchmaking.

Valerie I'm not matchmaking.

Kevin It's out of the question.

Valerie Of course it is. (*Pause*) But they would be good for each other. He needs someone like Lucy. And she's been very lonely since John died.

Kevin No one's that lonely! She's your friend. Why pick on her?

Valerie I'm not picking on her.

Kevin Have you forgotten how many times he's been engaged? He had that ring on a string. It's always been his ambition to marry money.

Valerie He never found the right woman.

Kevin He never found the right bank account. John Myers was a decent, honest man. A pillar of the church and a member of the Rotary. He didn't prepare Lucy for someone like Victor.

Valerie He'd have to tell her the truth …

Kevin Then we're safe on both counts. He couldn't tell the truth and she couldn't face it.

Valerie Sh!

Victor and Lucy enter from the garden

Victor (*as he enters*) ... and there by the bed sat my faithful mongoose, covered in blood, the snake dead at his feet, looking up at me as if to say, "sleep on, gentle master". And I swear, if a mongoose could smile, he was smiling ...
Lucy He must have been very fond of you.
Victor He was.
Valerie (*panicking*) I must get dinner.
Lucy Let me help you, Val. (*She smiles*) After all, we have another place to set ...

Lucy and Valerie exit

Victor limps back to the desk and sits. He catches Kevin's suspicious gaze

Victor Kevin, I want to ask you something as a friend ...
Kevin I haven't got it.
Victor Got what?
Kevin Money. I'm still cleaned out from last time.
Victor This isn't about money, Kevin.
Kevin It isn't?
Victor There are other things. I've just experienced a moment of blinding clarity. A moment the Japanese have a word for. A moment when you see your future life for the next seven years — all in a second.
Kevin Seven years?
Victor Yes.
Kevin (*anxiously*) I wasn't in it, was I?
Victor Not you. Lucy.
Kevin What!
Victor I'm in love.
Kevin You can't be.
Victor It only takes a second, Kev. I never thought it would happen again.
Kevin You mean after the nun?
Victor Blind fate has struck again.
Kevin Not so blind. It's the money, isn't it?
Victor (*innocently*) Is there money?
Kevin She's a wealthy woman. I'm sure one walk round the rose bed would have established that.

Victor Then she's not a widow struggling on a fixed income and facing an uncertain future?

Kevin No!

Victor That makes it more important that I talk to you.

Kevin Me?

Victor I wondered if you could see any snags.

Kevin I can see a few. You've been in prison — you're out of work — you haven't any money — you've told her a pack of lies — and you've got a bad leg.

Victor Yes, but apart from that.

Kevin There's no apart from that!

Victor What about the good points?

Kevin There aren't any.

Victor (*slyly*) There's one as far as you're concerned ...

Kevin What's that?

Victor Doesn't she live in Surrey?

Kevin Yes. Big house, must be worth a million.

Victor Well, Surrey's a long way from here ...

Kevin Oh no! If you think I'm going to stand by and let this happen. I may be an estate agent but I have principles. I believe in a full and frank disclosure. I have never recommended a run-down property without pointing out the drawbacks — the dry rot — the rising damp — the smell of the drains...

Victor The smell of the drains? Is that how you see me?

Kevin Yes.

Victor Well, let me point out one or two other good points. I do have money. It's a numbered account in a Swiss bank. Unfortunately, there's a problem.

Kevin You can't remember the number.

Victor I'm tied to the Swiss franc at the moment.

Kevin What a pity.

Victor And I do have work — my writing. When the book takes off ——

Kevin What book?

Victor takes a manuscript from the desk. Kevin stares in surprise

Victor I finished it in prison. I'm very excited about it. I read some of it to Val before you came home. She was speechless.

Kevin Then we've nothing to worry about. We just wait until you've sold the film rights.

Victor You don't believe me? It's a potential bestseller. Listen. (*He opens the manuscript. Reading*) "Mark Tempest confronted Amanda Merrydew in the vestry. There was no pity in his thin smile. He seized her brutally by the wrist. 'I must arrange these flowers'. But the words were stifled on her lips by a fierce kiss. Outside she could hear her husband leading the choir in Evensong. The organ rose in a crescendo of sound and she was aware of the roses being crushed against her bare skin and Mark's sardonic sneer. Her head began to swim and she caught the tang of his aftershave as they slid beneath the vestry table ..."

Silence

Kevin Vestry table?
Victor Yes.
Kevin Is it all like that?
Victor It gets better.

He hands the manuscript to Kevin

Read anywhere you like. You're instantly gripped.
Kevin (*reading*) "Mark took her in his arms." (*He breaks off*) He's doing it again! (*Reading*) "She felt her face pressed against his rough tweed jacket. The sun cascaded into a thousand stars and the petals of the geraniums floated down into her startled eyes ..." (*He breaks off*) Geraniums?
Victor She was potting geraniums whilst her husband was mowing the lawns.
Kevin Her husband? The vicar?
Victor Yes.
Kevin The vicar's out there mowing the lawns whilst they're in the greenhouse — and he's pressing her face against his rough tweed jacket?
Victor Right.
Kevin Is it a comedy?
Victor No.
Kevin But wouldn't he see them?
Victor That's my point. Mark Tempest would dare anything for the woman he loves.
Kevin Are you sure it's not a comedy?
Victor When the vicar discovers Amanda's infidelity and hangs himself from his own bell rope — certainly not. (*Pause*) Well, what do you think?
Kevin It's absolute rubbish.
Victor You don't like it?
Kevin No.

Victor I must say that's been the general reaction.

Kevin There's no reality. No one would act like Mark Tempest. He's not real.

Victor Yes, he is.

Kevin Well, I've never met any one like him.

Victor You're standing in front of him.

Kevin You? Well, you're not pressing Lucy against your rough tweed jacket — not while I'm mowing the lawn. And you'll have a long wait before that book's published. And in the meantime you're not living at my expense. Your trouble, Victor, is that you don't live in the real world. You're not Mark Tempest — and she's not Amanda Merrydew. You should try a little honesty for a change — especially with Lucy.

Victor (*doubtfully*) You mean tell her the truth?

Kevin Well, don't look like that — some people do it all the time.

Victor (*hesitating*) Not even a few white lies?

Kevin Certainly not.

Victor Perhaps you're right. The truth? It's an old trick but it just might work. Make a full and frank disclosure like the honest estate agent. That gives me an idea. I could work for you.

Kevin What!

Victor Just until my currency problems are sorted out. I can sell, you know that.

Kevin (*hastily*) That's not necessary, Victor. Houses are selling themselves these days.

Victor Then I could do your paperwork — answer the phone — all the menial jobs. I'm not proud. I could make life easier for you...

Kevin That won't be necessary.

The phone rings on the desk. Victor snatches it up

Victor I've got it, Kev. (*Into the phone*) Hello? Yes. Can I take a message? ... You've decided on Greenacres. An excellent choice. ... Yes. I know it well. It's the house next to the crematorium ... yes. (*Pause*) Hello? Hello? That's strange — they've rung off ...

Kevin gives a long, low groan

CURTAIN

SCENE 2

The same. Three weeks later. Midday

As the CURTAIN *rises, Kevin enters, throwing down his coat and looking vengeful. He sees the walking stick leaning by the desk. He crosses and snatches it up*

Kevin Ha! Got him. Val!

Valerie enters looking puzzled

Valerie What's the matter?
Kevin He forgot his stick. I knew there was nothing wrong with him.
Valerie He certainly seems to have improved.
Kevin Improved! He's been in my sock drawer too often for a man who can barely walk.
Valerie You don't begrudge him your socks, surely?
Kevin He comes into our bedroom without knocking. We could be doing anything.
Valerie (*tartly*) Not in the week, Kevin.
Kevin This house isn't big enough for both of us, Val.
Valerie Well, it's not as if he's here all the time. He's usually out with Lucy.
Kevin Yes, he's spending a fortune on her. How does he do it?
Valerie He uses credit cards. He hops from one to another.
Kevin He'll hop once too often. There'll be a reckoning — then what's going to happen?
Valerie I don't know.
Kevin There'll be a caper.
Valerie He doesn't do things like that.
Kevin Doesn't he? What about the map of Sierra Leone and a fortune in uncut diamonds that looked strangely like bath crystals? Remember that? And what about the dating agency? He never had enough clients so he put everyone on the books, including your mother — and me! When I pointed out I was engaged to you he said, "What's wrong with a night out"! And what about your poor mother? She arrived on her date just in time for his funeral — she was chased down the street by the widow. And when she came back, justifiably distressed, all he could say was, "Did they say anything about a subscription?".
Valerie You're getting agitated again, Kevin. You know you shouldn't talk about Victor on an empty stomach — it gives you indigestion. I'll cut you some sandwiches. Why don't you go into the conservatory and transplant some seedlings?

Kevin I don't want to transplant seedlings! I want him out of here.
Valerie You've never liked my brother, have you?
Kevin Don't say "my brother" like that.
Valerie Why not?
Kevin Because then I know you're going to take his side.
Valerie He was wonderful to me when Father left us.
Kevin (*sighing*) I know.
Valerie He was the breadwinner at sixteen. He was always there to pick me up when I fell. And he saved me from drowning at Broadstairs — don't forget that.
Kevin I can't — you won't let me. But just refresh my memory regarding the incident. Hadn't he pushed you in first?
Valerie He still saved me from drowning.

Valerie exits

Kevin (*shouting after her*) Well, if he'd been my brother I'd have fought him off and gone out with the tide!

Victor enters and stares curiously at Kevin

Victor Talking to yourself, Kevin? You'd better watch that.

Kevin picks up the stick and waves it under Victor's nose

Is something the matter?
Kevin You forgot your faithful old hickory, Victor.
Victor Throw it away, Kev.
Kevin What?
Victor I don't need it.
Kevin Why?
Victor Acupuncture. Little place off the high street. Twenty needles in the thigh — ten in the calf. Feel a new man. (*He crosses and places a jewellery box on the desk. He stands back*) Know what this is, Kev?
Kevin Well, it's too big for the ring.
Victor The ring?
Kevin The pigeon ruby with homing instincts.
Victor I don't understand.
Kevin She'll be leaving soon — isn't this time to spring the trap? Propose marriage and solve your money problems? Well, when the vicar says is there any just cause or impediment, I'll be there with bells on.
Victor Kevin, what makes you think I have money problems?

Kevin Because you're wearing my socks.

Victor A temporary embarrassment.

Kevin I know the feeling.

Victor I wouldn't propose to Lucy — she hardly knows me.

Kevin Oh. (*He hesitates*) Then you haven't …?

Victor Haven't what?

Kevin You know …

Victor No! Certainly not. She's barely out of mourning. This is just a little gift to show how much I value her friendship. (*He opens the box*)

Kevin (*peering in*) Where did you get it?

Victor Rogers' — in the Market Place.

Kevin He has some nice stuff. Those diamonds look almost real.

Victor They are real. Look at the price tag.

Kevin (*gasping*) Ten thousand pounds! But you haven't got ten thousand pounds.

Victor It's on approval.

Kevin They let that out of the shop on approval? I don't believe it.

Victor I gave the manager an excellent reference.

Kevin You must have done. Who was it?

Victor You.

Kevin I haven't got ten thousand pounds! I'm still recovering from Rockfast Investments.

Victor Calm down, Kevin. You won't have to find the money. It'll be back in the shop by the afternoon.

Kevin I thought you were going to give it to Lucy?

Victor I am. But she won't accept it.

Kevin She won't?

Victor Put yourself in her place. She already says I've spent too much money on her. She can hardly accept such an expensive gift from a man she hardly knows.

Kevin I suppose not.

Victor She'll reject it gently but firmly. Lucy's that sort of person.

Kevin But, Victor — if she's going to reject it gently but firmly — why give it in the first place?

Victor Because she's a woman, Kevin. When she opens that box there'll be a sharp intake of breath. Then she'll say, "I can't take this, Victor — you can't buy your way into my affections." But her cheek will be flushed and her eye will be bright. She'll call me a fool but her voice will be gentle. She'll see me in a different light — someone who doesn't give a fig for money — who's prepared to make the big gesture. And it won't have cost me a penny.

Kevin (*admiringly*) You crafty devil.

Victor Just a man who understands women, Kevin. You need to be subtle. When you're going to throw a brick at a cat, you don't make any sudden movements — you move by stealth — and then bang — the cat doesn't know what hit it. And it's the same with the opposite sex ...

Lucy enters

Lucy Oh. Am I interrupting something?
Kevin No, I was just going to transplant a few seedlings ...

Kevin exits diffidently into the conservatory

Victor Lucy, there's something I want to say to you. As you know I'm a man of few words — a rough fellow — more familiar with the campfire than the drawing-room. Unused to the company of women.
Lucy (*smiling*) Except for the nun.
Victor There was always the rosary between us.
Lucy And there was no one else in all those years?
Victor I was far from civilization — amongst primitive tribes. Oh, the natives adored me — the white man whose stick spoke thunder — but it was difficult to get close to them. In fact you're the first unattached woman I've been with in years who's not covered in rancid animal fat.
Lucy I suppose that does give me an advantage.
Victor You have been happy these last weeks, Lucy?
Lucy I've had a wonderful time.
Victor I thought so. And that gives me the courage to speak out — to reach for the sacred chalice — to knock, albeit timidly, on the gates of love...
Lucy (*smiling*) Is that how they talk around the campfire?
Victor A man can dream. He can look into the flames and see a greener land, softer skies, and a gentle woman cutting flowers for the house ...

Victor realizes that Lucy has turned away and that her shoulders are shaking gently

(*Frowning*) Are you laughing?
Lucy I'm sorry, I didn't mean to.
Victor You're right — I must seem a comic figure.
Lucy No.

Victor My trouble is I've spent so many years pursuing wealth I've forgotten how to talk to a woman. Perhaps this small gift will express my feelings better...

Victor hands her the box

Lucy No, I couldn't. You've spent enough on me already.
Victor Please.

She opens the box. She gives a sharp intake of breath and takes out a diamond bracelet. Victor smiles in anticipation

Lucy Victor, it's beautiful. It must have been terribly expensive. (*Seeing the tag*) It is terribly expensive!
Victor Damn! Did I leave the price tag on?
Lucy Yes. But it's worth every penny. I've never seen anything so beautiful. Look at those diamonds. What can I say?

Victor begins to grow uneasy

Victor I see. How could I be so insensitive?
Lucy What?
Victor I know what you're trying to say. You can't accept it. You can't accept such an expensive gift from a man you hardly know.
Lucy (*hesitating*) Well, I wasn't trying to say that exactly ...
Victor Don't try and spare my feelings, Lucy. You have every right to be offended.
Lucy But I'm not offended.
Victor You're not? Don't you feel ... bought?
Lucy No.
Victor If you want to return it, Lucy — I'll be hurt but I'll understand. And perhaps one day, when we know each other better, you'll accept this gift in the right spirit.
Lucy But I don't want to hurt your feelings.
Victor (*desperately*) My feelings don't come into it. You must follow your instincts.
Lucy (*after a pause*) Well, my instinct is to keep it.
Victor What?
Lucy I can't wait to show it to Valerie.

Lucy exits excitedly

Victor sags slightly

Kevin enters gloomily from the conservatory

Kevin So she didn't return it gently but firmly?
Victor No.
Kevin I thought you understood women?
Victor I forgot that where diamonds are concerned women become slightly deranged.
Kevin But you were going to return it this afternoon.
Victor I know. So when she comes back say you don't like it.
Kevin But I do like it.
Victor Then perhaps you'd like to pay for it?
Kevin I don't like it that much.
Victor Don't forget whose name I gave as a reference …
Kevin I don't like it at all. But why should my opinion matter?
Victor Because you're a man, Kevin. Why do you think women wear jewellery? To attract men. If it doesn't attract you — it may make her think.

Valerie and Lucy enter excitedly

Valerie Kevin, just look at the bracelet Victor's bought for Lucy — isn't it beautiful?
Kevin (*looking at the bracelet without enthusiasm*) Hm …
Valerie (*staring*) Don't you like it?
Kevin Not really.

Valerie and Lucy look surprised

Valerie Don't be silly, Kevin.
Victor No, let Kevin have his say. He's entitled to have an opinion. Don't you agree, Lucy?
Lucy Well, yes, but it doesn't really matter. I like it.
Victor Of course. And why should Kevin's opinion, honestly held, concern you? After all, he's looking at it as a man.
Valerie Yes, a mean one. When we became engaged my diamond was the smallest in the shop. I kept thinking it had fallen out.
Kevin It's only my opinion.
Valerie Why do you have to belittle everything my brother does?
Victor I don't think Kevin's concerned about the price. He just doesn't like it.
Valerie No one's asking him to wear it.
Victor Are you suggesting it's a shade vulgar, Kevin?
Kevin Yes.

Lucy What!

Victor I must say I hadn't seen it like that.

Lucy Neither had I.

Victor Still, we must respect Kevin's opinion.

Valerie Why? He only goes to the jewellers to have his watch cleaned.

Victor I think Kevin's pointing out something we've all missed. Exploitation.

Lucy Exploitation?

Victor Of the poor devils who dug those diamonds out of the ground on starvation wages — collapsing from fatigue and malnutrition — just for them to adorn pampered Western women. That's what you're getting at, isn't it, Kevin?

Kevin Yes.

Victor I must say until Kevin spoke out I hadn't thought of it like that. I suppose you think something simple in gold would be more appropriate, Kevin?

Kevin Yes.

Valerie Why don't you shut up, Kevin?

Lucy That's all right, Val. I don't want something simple in gold. I'm sorry for the poor men collapsing and everything but the diamonds are out of the ground now — we can't put them back. Now I'm going to see what it looks like with my red dress...

Lucy exits

Valerie (*rounding on Kevin*) How dare you talk to Lucy like that?

Kevin What did I say?

Valerie It's one thing to have an opinion — it's another to be rude. Did you ever think of Victor's feelings? I just wish someone thought enough of me to buy me an expensive bracelet.

Valerie slams out

Kevin gives a low groan

Kevin Did you hear that?

Victor Perhaps you were a little outspoken, Kevin.

Kevin What are we going to do? You were supposed to return it by this afternoon.

Victor Keep calm, Kevin. Let me think. (*He paces about the room, then stops*) Suppose I was to say that the bracelet was second hand. That it once belonged to the unhappy Grisley family.

Kevin (*staring*) Grisley family?

Victor That the bracelet had brought the family endless bad luck. That Josiah Grisley had acquired the bracelet just before the Indian mutiny. He was the one they found at the bottom of the Black Hole of Calcutta — having gone in first to get a seat. Since then the family have known nothing but misfortune. Having learned of this — and fearing for Lucy's safety …

Kevin is slowly shaking his head

No?

Kevin No, Victor.

Victor Perhaps you have a better idea?

Kevin I have. It's quite simple. You have to quarrel with her.

Victor Quarrel with her?

Kevin Then she'll give it back.

Victor Are you sure?

Kevin Engaged couples do it all the time. They get tense and irritable with each other — the next thing the engagement ring is flying through the air.

Victor You mean she'd throw the bracelet back at me?

Kevin That's right.

Victor But if I quarrel with her, what was the point of giving her the bracelet in the first place?

Kevin You can make it up later — once the bracelet's safely back in the shop.

Victor Has this ever happened to you, Kevin?

Kevin Oh, yes. Val was always throwing her engagement ring back at me. I'd stand there like a slip fielder some nights.

Victor Why was that?

Kevin You know how it was when you're engaged — the pressures …

Victor What pressures?

Kevin (*awkwardly*) Not being married — and not being single — feeling frustrated. And Val wouldn't — never did. Would have liked to have done — but she didn't. Anyone who says she did — you can tell them, she didn't…

Victor Didn't what?

Kevin She wouldn't — not Val. Saved herself.

Victor What for?

Kevin Me.

Victor But you were there.

Kevin For the honeymoon. And I'd get tense.

Victor I'm not surprised. You were engaged for five years, Kevin.

Valerie enters looking perturbed

Valerie Mr Turner, from the bank, is here! He's waiting in the hall!

Kevin What! (*He panics*) Turner from the bank. We can't be overdrawn, surely. What does he want with me?

Valerie He doesn't want to see you — he wants to see Victor.

Kevin What?

Victor It's all right, Kev. I sent for him.

Kevin You sent for Turner! No one sends for Turner. Why?

Victor I wish to extend my credit facilities — possibly an overdraft — or a bank loan. Would you send him through, Val.

Valerie exits looking flustered

Kevin Turner's come here! I have to make an appointment to see him. I've only just got on his Christmas card list. I was hoping he'd put me up for the Rotary. And you've got him standing in the hall!

Victor Don't panic, Kevin. I've always been on the friendliest terms with the bank. I just want to continue the special relationship I had with old Truscott.

Kevin But he's nothing like old Truscott. He's big and ugly. He played rugby for Bentham Old Boys and the Saracens. He still thinks he's in the scrum. He's called Tank. He has a grip like a vice. If he shakes hands with you, count your fingers, you could find two missing.

Victor (*smiling*) Stop gibbering, Kevin. I have done my homework.

Tank Turner enters. He is a big, robust man about fifty. He is a bit of a buffoon, self-important and serious

Ah, Mr Turner, good of you to come.

Tank (*ominously*) I thought I ought to under the circumstances ...

Tank extends a formidable hand. Victor extends his own then wafts it in the direction of Kevin

Victor You know my brother-in-law, Kevin?

Tank grips Kevin's hand. Kevin buckles at his knees

Tank Kevin ...?

Kevin (*gasping*) Bunce.

Tank Oh, yes. Thought you looked familiar.

Victor Weren't you going to transplant some seedlings, Kevin?

Kevin Yes, I was ...

Kevin exits into the conservatory flexing his fingers

Tank You know, I can never remember that fellow's name.
Victor No one can. Don't worry about it. Can I get you a drink?

A glimpse of Kevin glaring around the door, before he disappears

Tank Not at the moment. I'd prefer to get down to business. I've extracted your account details from the computer, Mr Blake — I have them here.
Victor That's what I like about your bank — efficiency.
Tank Quite. Unfortunately you appear to be overdrawn by the sum of sixty thousand pounds and fifty-six p.
Victor And accuracy.
Tank What?
Victor I like that. Gives me confidence.
Tank The sum has been outstanding for several years with mounting interest. That's why I called personally.
Victor And friendliness.
Tank Pardon?
Victor It is known as the friendly bank?
Tank Well, yes.
Victor That's why I came to you. I took your friendliness into consideration.
Tank The point is this, what are you going to do about it?
Victor Pay it off. It's been outstanding far too long.
Tank (*relieved*) Good.

Victor pours out the contents of his wallet on to the desk and begins to make out a cheque. Tank stares

Isn't that one of our cheque books?
Victor Yes.
Tank I can't accept that.
Victor Aren't they any good?
Tank Mr Blake, you're paying us back with our own money.
Victor Not if you lend it to me first.
Tank Lend it to you?
Victor It's not for me to teach you your business, Mr Turner. But if you made me a secured loan of, say, seventy thousand pounds — I could pay off the overdraft and have ten thousand to invest in a rather attractive proposition. We could forget the fifty p.
Tank But, Mr Blake, you have no security — you appear to be reduced to living with your brother-in-law. You have no means and no money.

Victor I see. You only loan money to people who've got it. Isn't that rather a waste of time?

Tank But we have loaned you money. Sixty thousand pounds. I don't think it's unreasonable for Head Office to expect it back. (*He picks up the cheque book and credit cards from the desk*) I'm afraid I'll have to retain this cheque book — and your cards — since they'll be of no further use to you. I'm sorry.

Victor Don't worry, Mr Turner — I've faced adversity before. That's one thing Benthams taught me. Never to give up.

Tank (*staring*) One moment. Did you say Benthams?

Victor Yes.

Tank You were at Benthams?

Victor Well, yes.

Tank What a coincidence. So was I.

Victor Really?

Tank Before your time of course.

Victor Wait a minute. Turner ... not *the* Tank Turner?

Tank You've heard of me?

Victor When I played for the first fifteen Tank Turner was still something of a legend.

Tank You played for the first fifteen?

Victor Wing-and-three quarter. Bodger Blake.

Tank Bodger ... I don't seem to recall...

Victor I was only there briefly — before going to Oxford.

Tank Oxford.

Victor But they all remembered you, Tank. They said you were the best forward the school ever had.

Tank (*excitedly*) Who said that? Was it Pop Askew?

Victor Who else? He said Tank Turner was someone we could all look up to.

Tank Pop said that?

Victor I never thought the day would come when I'd meet the man behind the legend — and be disappointed.

Tank Disappointed?

Victor Not because he turned his back on a fellow Benthamian.

Tank I'm not turning my back, exactly.

Victor I expected to meet the great Tank Turner and what did I find? A man frightened of Head Office.

Tank Who said I was frightened?

Victor I wonder what Pop Askew would say if he were here now? I remember his last words to me before I went up to Oxford. He shook hands and his eyes become clouded in thought and he said: "Bodger, remember ... life is a great game of rugby. You have to decide when to run with the ball and when to kick for touch. And when life becomes a scrum — hold fast to your friends. Remember the great referee in the sky is watching — and he can see on the blind side. And when you hear that final whistle and reach that distant line, it doesn't matter if you've won or lost, only if you've played the game." Are you playing the game, Tank?

Tank But I've no alternative ——

Victor I thought about you the day I played against the Springboks ...

Tank You played against the Springboks?

Victor When I was at Oxford.

Kevin peers incredulously around the door and then retreats

I was facing the last twenty minutes with a broken collarbone. I thought: what would Tank Turner do in this situation? And I played on. I thought one day I'll tell him that but then, I didn't expect to meet a bank clerk ...

Tank But you don't understand. You said a secured loan. Where's your security?

Victor smiles and takes out a crumpled piece of paper. He hands it to Turner. Turner studies it

It looks like a map.

Victor Not just a map — the key to a fortune.

Tank What?

Victor I didn't waste my time whilst I was out in Africa. I was a soldier of fortune — moving from one turbulent frontier to the next. I've seen sights that would freeze your blood, Tank. Terrible sights. Ever seen a man covered in pastry and cooked over an open fire? I have. But during all those privations I always kept my eye open for the main chance. It was during this time that I met Mad Henry.

Tank Mad Henry?

Victor A legendary figure out there. He was sick with malaria when I met him — already dying. I carried him for miles on my back over the trackless waste until we came to water. It seems strange talking about it here in this mundane suburban drawing-room with its simulated log fire.

Another furious glance from Kevin at the door before he disappears again

But it seems as if it were only yesterday. His eyes were burning with fever — the end was near — then he thrust this map into my hand and croaked one last word — "diamonds".

Tank Diamonds?

Victor This map shows a point where the frontiers of Sierra Leone —
Guinea — and Liberia meet. Well-known diamond country. I could
get the mineral rights for ten thousand pounds. They're simple peasant
farmers — they don't like diamonds getting in the way of the ground-
nuts.

Tank You seriously expect me to advance ten thousand pounds on the
strength of this piece of paper?

Victor It could be worth millions.

Tank Millions!

Victor What's the matter, Tank — frightened of being rich?

Tank But Mad Henry — doesn't that imply...he was mad?

Victor (*laughing*) They called him mad when he said he'd found the
elephants' graveyard. They called him mad when he said there was oil
in Madagascar. Mad Henry made and lost more fortunes than any man
alive. And I'm prepared to believe his dying words — even without
these ... (*He looks around cautiously and takes a pouch from around
his neck, pours contents on desk*)

Tank What are they?

Victor Uncut diamonds.

Tank They don't look like diamonds.

Victor Uncut diamonds don't — that's how you can tell they're
diamonds. If they looked like diamonds — they wouldn't be. No,
when these little beauties are cut and polished they could be worth
fifty thousand.

Tank But then why don't you simply sell these?

Victor (*smiling*) Sell them? Before we've got the rights? You're being
naïve, even for a bank manager. If the big diamond consortiums were
to find out, our very lives could be in danger. You're in danger even
knowing of this map's existence. But then you've never flinched from
danger, have you, Tank? Remember what Pop Askew said? There's a
time to run with the ball and there's a time to kick for touch. This is
the time to run with the ball.

Tank (*hesitating*) Millions, did you say?

Victor At a conservative estimate ...

Tank (*shaking his head*) No, I couldn't risk the bank's money.

Victor (*coldly*) I see.

Tank But I might risk my own ... with the proper safeguards.

Victor I knew I was right about you, Tank.

Tank And I'm sure I'm right about you, Bodger. After all, I've never
known a Bentham man do anything dishonourable.

Victor Quite. Now if you could make out your cheque for ten thousand
— time is of the essence.

Tank sits at the desk and takes out his cheque book

And if you could return mine — it would help to move things along …

Tank takes out Victor's cheque book and cards. He hesitates

Tank You will be sensible, Bodger? No large withdrawals for the time being. You will be frugal?
Victor Of course I'll be frugal. I couldn't live any cheaper than I am doing. That's why I'm dossing down here.

Another indignant brief appearance at the door from Kevin

Lucy enters excitedly from the hall wearing her red dress

Lucy What do you think, Victor? Doesn't it look wonderful?
Victor (*hastily*) Lucy, this is Mr Turner, from the bank.
Lucy Hello. I've just been trying on Victor's present. (*Holding up her wrist*) Isn't he extravagant? It cost thousands. All diamonds. He's such a dear.

Turner who is about to hand Victor his cheque book, stops, returns it to his pocket. He rises in silence and exits

Victor slumps for a moment in defeat

What a strange man. (*She whirls around the room*) Doesn't it go beautifully with this dress?

Victor studies her for a moment

Victor Yes … (*He crosses, takes hold of her and turns her towards him*) Then what about a little appreciation …
Lucy What?
Victor Don't be coy, Lucy. This maiden modesty doesn't become you. Let's face it, you've been in mourning longer than Queen Victoria.
Lucy Victor, have you been drinking?
Victor What if I have? If I want a drink — I'll take a drink. I'll drink myself stupid if I feel like it. No Sunday school teacher's going to change me, Lucy.
Lucy I wasn't trying to change you.
Victor Yes, you were. You're quite the little reformer, aren't you? Well don't bang your tambourine at me. I was forged out there, under the blazing sun, with the heat, and the flies, and the disease. We were

free-booters — soldiers of fortune. We drank our way through every frontier town in Africa. And if that shocks you then I suggest you settle down and marry the curate. Because where I come from, girlie — that bracelet means you're my woman.

Lucy What! (*She draws back and tugs at the bracelet*)

Victor That's right — throw it back in my face. What are you waiting for?

Lucy (*hesitating*) Perhaps you're right.

Victor What?

Lucy Perhaps I've been dishonest.

Victor No!

Lucy Perhaps I'm clinging to the past.

Victor If you want to cling to the past — cling to it. Go on — throw it in my face.

Lucy How can I blame you.

Victor Blame me!

Lucy It's just that you're so different from John. He was such a quiet, sober man. He never raised his voice to me.

Victor Didn't he? Well, I'm tired of hearing about your wonderful husband and your perfect marriage. What did he die of — boredom?

Lucy You brute! (*She snatches the bracelet off her wrist*)

Victor That's right. I'm a brute. What are you going to do about it?

Lucy (*hesitating*) I know why you're doing this.

Victor You do?

Lucy You're madly jealous. Jealous of a ghost. You gave me the bracelet and I gave you nothing in return — not even a kiss. You've every right to be angry.

Victor No I haven't. I'm a brute.

He seizes her and kisses her savagely. She pulls away and regards him

Lucy God, Victor — you're so masterful …

She dashes from the room

Kevin enters from the conservatory

They stare at each other blankly. Kevin gives a low groan

CURTAIN

ACT II

Scene 1

The same. The following afternoon

As the Curtain *rises, Kevin is on the phone*

Kevin I can assure you, Mr Blake will be returning the bracelet later this afternoon, or possibly tomorrow morning — Monday at the latest. … Yes, I realize it must be awkward for you. … Yes, I'll tell him when he gets in … bye. (*He puts the phone down and sighs*)

Valerie enters

Valerie Is something the matter?

Kevin Your brother's the matter.

Valerie Don't say "your brother" like that. I know there's going to be trouble when you say that.

Kevin Now you know how I feel when you say "my brother".

Valerie What's he done?

Kevin Nothing. That's the trouble. When is he going to get a job? He's been through my sock drawer. He's wearing my underwear, my ties. Thank God my suits don't fit him. And he spends hours in the bathroom — he's using all the soap. And he's eating enough for two. Did you see the way he cleared his plate last night? I thought he was feeding something under the table.

Valerie He has to build up his strength. He has been on a prison diet.

Kevin It's not bread and water anymore, Val. It's like Butlins — and he's treating this place the same. When are we going to see some money?

Valerie He says he's hoping to get an advance on his book.

Kevin Mark Tempest and Amanda Merrydew cavorting amongst the geraniums? He has more chance of being struck by lightning. And in the meantime how does he propose to live?

Valerie He must have some money. He bought Lucy that very expensive bracelet.

Kevin (*after a pause*) Val, he didn't buy it.

Valerie What do you mean?

Kevin It's on approval. He thought she wouldn't accept it. It was another caper.

Valerie But why?

Kevin To impress her — so that she wouldn't think he was after her money — which he certainly is. He intends to sweep her off her feet, marry her, and pay off his debts. And the way things are going, I can see it happening.

Valerie It won't. I won't let it happen. Unless he gets a job and proves himself — I'm going to ask him to leave.

Kevin If you mean that I suggest you go down to *The George*, where he's holding court with his drinking cronies, and tell him ——

Victor enters

Kevin breaks off. There's a guilty silence

Victor Is something the matter? You look troubled, little sister.

Valerie turns away

I knew it. This is something I dreaded. I'm causing dissension. I'm coming between you. Perhaps it would be better if I looked for some rented accommodation in the town ... (*He pauses hopefully*)

There's a cold silence

I shall be able to afford something modest — now I've got a job.

Valerie turns in surprise

Valerie You've got a job?

Victor Well, it's as good as mine — they virtually promised. I'm going into sewage.

Valerie Sewage!

Kevin (*smiling*) Sewage?

Victor Yes. There are quite a few people after it but I stand a very good chance. I'm the right height.

Valerie Height?

Victor For wading. The other applicants are rather short — and during the winter floods you could be up to your ears in it.

Valerie In what?

Victor Effluent. Oh, just one thing, Valerie — whilst I'm staying here — and it is quite important — they did ask. Will you be prepared to wash my overalls?

Valerie Overalls! Victor, you're not wearing overalls?

Victor I have to — and waders.

Valerie Waders! Why can't you get a clean job?

Victor Dear Sis, I had a clean job and what happened? There was a slump in property and I ended up in prison. Let's face it — sewage is about all I'm good for. (*Brokenly*) I'm not fit for anything else.

Valerie Victor, you can't take that job.

Kevin (*enjoying himself*) Oh, I don't know, it could be a rich experience.

Valerie I don't know why you find it so amusing, Kevin. You say he spends too much time in the bathroom as it is — and think of the soap.

Kevin They'll probably provide him with soap — strong carbolic.

Valerie My brother's not going into sewage — that's final. What would our friends say?

Kevin I suppose it would cause a stink ...

Valerie You're not going to take that job, Victor. You're better than that. You have to believe in yourself. You have to wait for the right opportunity. In the meantime, if you're short of money Kevin will lend you some.

Kevin What!

Valerie exits

Kevin sighs and takes a cheque book from the drawer

I knew it would come to this. How much?

Victor Should we say a thousand?

Kevin throws the pen over his shoulder

Kevin We'll say no such thing. Why not ask for the moon and the stars. Perhaps you'd like the gold fillings from my teeth and for Val to pawn her jewellery?

Victor That won't be necessary. If you're not prepared to invest in the future ...

Kevin What future?

Victor A thousand lottery tickets.

Kevin What?

Victor The numbers based on my father's infallible system at roulette. The one he used at the tables in Monte Carlo.

Kevin Victor, your father died a bankrupt. He was out of touch with reality and so are you. You are not Mark Tempest pursuing Amanda Merrydew around the vestry table. You're not Bodger Blake, late of Benthams and terror of the scrum. There is no Mad Henry or a fortune in uncut diamonds. You were very near to getting your collar felt. Only my concern for my good name prevented me from speaking out. You have no chance of getting any money out of me — and I'm going to tell Valerie that.

Kevin exits into hall

Victor sighs and slumps defeated into the high-backed chair. He turns his back to the room

A moment later Soapy Simpson enters cautiously from the terrace. He is in his thirties, good looking in a raffish sort of way. He has a spotted handkerchief around his neck and a faintly bohemian air. He is carrying a canvas which he leans against the wall

He crosses to the cocktail cabinet and pours himself a scotch, at the same time he slips a silver cigarette box into his pocket

Victor becomes aware of his presence and turns towards him

Victor Perhaps you'd care to try the malt? It's an excellent blend, specially prepared for the discerning drinker.

Soapy wheels round

Soapy I do apologize, sir. I came over faint in the street — I couldn't make anyone hear and I ... (*He stops*) Strike me! It can't be. It's you, Blakey.

Victor What? (*He studies him*) Good Lord! It's Soapy Simpson. What are you doing here?

Soapy I was in the neighbourhood, purveying a few pictures from door to door — and I called here. I didn't expect to find you.

Victor But you were a skilled cracksman. What are you doing on the knocker? You were the Raffles of North London.

Soapy (*modestly*) I know, I still have the cuttings. "Silent and swift with the agility of a cat." *Daily Mail.* "Cool and cynical and elusive as a fox." *Daily Express.* "He fades into the darkness like a panther." *Daily Telegraph.*

Victor What happened to you?
Soapy I kept getting caught. So I decided to go straight.
Victor Really?

Victor takes the silver box from Soapy's pocket

Soapy Sorry, Blakey — I didn't know you were doing this place.
Victor (*indignantly*) I'm not! I live here.
Soapy Oh. You did say the malt? (*He pours himself a drink. He looks around*) You appear to be doing rather well. You wouldn't like to buy a picture — a rural landscape? (*He crosses and picks up the picture*)
Victor Let me see. I don't know much about art but I know what I like … (*He studies picture*) I like it. Those art classes have certainly paid off, Soapy.
Soapy They don't call me that these days. I mean who ever heard of an artist called Soapy Simpson? It's Seagrave.
Victor Seagrave?
Soapy Seagrave Simpson. See the signature?
Victor Very impressive.
Soapy You really like it?
Victor It's good — damned good. There's great feeling in this picture. It means something to you — a scene from your boyhood. I want to go there, Soapy — where is it?
Soapy I don't know. I got it off a chocolate box.
Victor Still, it's very authentic. A man who can handle a brush like this shouldn't be going from door to door … keep in touch. I may be able to do something for you …

Soapy realizes he's being moved gently towards the garden

Soapy You wouldn't be trying to get rid of me?
Victor No.
Soapy But I suppose my presence could be an embarrassment …
Victor Certainly not.
Soapy Then I'll stay. After all, it's your duty to support the struggling artist.
Victor Yes … but your presence would take a little explaining …
Soapy You could do it. Blakey. You always had a silver tongue. You persuaded me to take that top bunk when we were inside. Said it would be good for my asthma. I spent six months hanging up there like a bleeding bat — my back's never been the same … (*He takes another drink and makes himself comfortable*)

Kevin enters from the hall and stares incredulously

Victor Oh, Kevin, could I introduce ——
Kevin No! Certainly not! I suppose he's one of your drinking cronies from *The George*. Get him out of here.

Soapy pulls himself up with battered dignity

Soapy Sir, if I've unwittingly prevailed on your hospitality — forgive me. Please allow me to make small recompense. A fiver should cover the drink ... (*He throws a battered note on the desk. He moves to the french doors and stands affronted. He does not leave*)
Victor Seagrave, please forgive my brother-in-law for his intemperate outburst. His only excuse is that he doesn't know who you are.
Kevin What?

Soapy looks loftily over his shoulder

Victor (*hissing*) Do you realize what you've just done? You've insulted Seagrave Simpson.
Kevin Seagrave Simpson?
Victor Where have you been all these years? Seagrave Simpson, the artist, member of the Royal Academy, and court painter to Her Majesty.
Kevin (*impressed*) Her Majesty?
Victor I can't believe this has happened. You've never heard of Seagrave Simpson!
Kevin (*hesitating*) Well, I didn't say I hadn't heard of him. I'm not a philistine, Victor. But what's he doing here?
Victor Being insulted, Kevin.
Kevin Look, I'm sorry, Seagrave. Let me freshen your drink ...

Soapy turns and gives him a condescending nod

Victor I met Seagrave at *The George* and asked him back to authenticate a picture.
Kevin I didn't know you had a picture.

Victor motions towards canvas

Victor I didn't want to bring it out into the strong light — it could be valuable. I was hoping Seagrave would identify it as a genuine Simpson.

Kevin hands Soapy a large drink

Kevin I must apologize, Seagrave. It's just that I've been under considerable strain recently.

Victor You don't have to tell Seagrave that. He can see you've been under considerable strain. He's looking at you with the eye of an artist.

Soapy Not another word, Kevin. Let's drink to our friendship. (*He drains the glass and pours himself another*)

Victor begins to look worried

Kevin You must lead an interesting life.

Soapy I do.

Kevin What is she really like?

Soapy Who?

Kevin Her Majesty?

Soapy Her Majesty?

Kevin Have you painted her many times?

Soapy Oh, yes, many times.

Kevin Is she as regal as they say?

Soapy More so. But she's also a woman, Kevin — with an inner radiance I can't describe. And she dotes on me.

Victor (*hastily*) Perhaps you'd look at the picture, Seagrave ——

Soapy In fact, you could say, although I'm her subject, she is also mine.

Victor Er, well expressed, Seagrave.

Soapy It's those damned corgis I can't stand. They won't keep still for a minute.

Victor Seagrave, could you run your eye over this picture. Is it a genuine Simpson?

He hands the picture to Soapy who studies it solemnly

Soapy Let me see ... Yes ... Note the distinctive brush strokes. The clever use of light and shade. The hallmark of a genuine Simpson.

Kevin It looks familiar.

Soapy Do you like chocolate?

Victor (*quickly*) Of course it looks familiar. You feel as if you've been there. That's because it's so evocative. Well, congratulate me, Kevin, it must be worth a couple of thousand.

Soapy Five.

Kevin Good Lord!

Soapy Ten when I'm dead.

Kevin Ten! I didn't realize … I got a Ford Focus for that, only a year old. But what are you doing in these parts, Seagrave?

Soapy What am I doing in these parts?

Victor Seagrave has just finished a large canvas at Windsor — now he's taking a break. A little light sketching while he finds a new subject to paint.

Soapy Yes, I'm looking for a face full of character that will inspire me to even greater heights.

Victor Why are looking at Kevin like that, Seagrave?

Soapy What?

Victor He's looking at you, Kevin.

Kevin Is he?

Victor He's seen something. You've seen something in his face, haven't you, Seagrave?

Soapy silently raises his thumb and looks down it as if to judge Kevin's perspective

Soapy Yes…

Victor (*excitedly*) Kevin, he wants to paint you.

Kevin What!

Soapy That face has been lived in — used by life. It has known joy and sorrow. I must get it down on canvas.

Victor But Seagrave, do you have the time?

Soapy I have the time and my paints and brushes are to hand. I'll get them forthwith.

Soapy downs his drink and exits, a shade unsteadily, through the hall

Kevin (*anxiously*) Victor, I know it's a great compliment but how much will it cost?

Victor We're not going to quibble over money, are we, Kevin?

Kevin Yes.

Victor He may not even offer it to you.

Kevin What?

Victor He may wish to exhibit it.

Kevin Exhibit it?

Victor At the Royal Academy. It may be bought by some merchant banker as a hedge against inflation. You may end up in his dining-room.

Kevin I don't like the sound of that. After all, it is my picture.

Victor Well ethically, I suppose he should offer it to you first — at a nominal charge …

Kevin How nominal?

Victor I'd say a couple of thousand.

Kevin What!

Victor Money doesn't mean much to him.

Kevin I'm not surprised.

Victor And what are your friends going to say when they hear you've been painted by Seagrave Simpson?

Kevin I don't know.

Victor They'll be green with envy. They'll be begging you to join the Rotary, just to get an introduction. Above the mock Regency fireplace — with its simulated log effect and its fake Grecian vase will be something totally original. You, Kevin.

Kevin I hadn't thought of it like that.

Victor Now, why don't you go and freshen up? Because what you look like now, you'll look like for the next five hundred years.

Kevin (*impressed*) Five hundred years?

Victor That works out at about four pound a year.

Kevin exits in a daze

Victor crosses to the desk and begins to make financial calculations on a notepad

Soapy staggers through the french doors encumbered with easel, canvas, paints, etc.

Soapy (*looking around*) Has he gone?

Victor He'll be back. But before he comes, let's get things straight. First, I'll handle the money.

Soapy Right.

Victor Second, are you prepared to paint Kevin for a thousand pounds?

Soapy A thousand pounds! I'd paint the house for that.

Victor Then we're in business. And there'll be plenty of business around here. We'll have half the Rotary before long.

Soapy begins to assemble the easel

Soapy (*frowning*) The Rotary? But will they be good for the money? I went to one of their lunches once. Boiled beef and carrots — and a bottle of wine between six!

Victor They'll pay for this. (*Pause*) I suppose you can paint faces?

Soapy No problem. I'll have it done in half an hour.

Victor Don't do it too quickly. Spin it out. And flatter him.
Soapy Flatter him? That's going to be difficult. He's got a funny face.
Victor You may think he's got a funny face — he thinks he's handsome.

Lucy enters from the hall and regards them curiously

Lucy Oh, sorry — I didn't realize you had a visitor.
Victor Lucy, allow me to introduce Seagrave Simpson — the celebrated painter and member of the Royal Academy.
Soapy And painter to Her Majesty.
Victor And painter to Her Majesty. Lucy Myers.

Soapy advances leering. He takes her hand and kisses it. His eyes light on the bracelet

Soapy Charming ... would you like a drink? I'm having one.
Lucy Not at the moment.

She stares as Soapy pours the scotch unwittingly into a mixing jar

Are you going to paint someone?
Victor Yes, Kevin.
Lucy (*surprised*) Kevin. Why?
Soapy I've found something interesting in his face.
Lucy What was that?
Soapy I'm not sure.
Victor Seagrave wants to capture Kevin's sorrow.
Soapy I'm very good on sorrow. I just turn the mouth down.
Victor Isn't it fascinating, Lucy — hearing these insights from a master?
Lucy (*doubtfully*) Yes. I must confess I don't think I've seen any of your work.
Victor It's mostly in private hands.
Soapy But you can cop a look at this one.

Soapy shows Lucy the finished picture

Autumn scene.

Lucy studies the picture

Lucy Isn't that a Constable?

Soapy whirls around

Soapy Where?

Victor Full marks for spotting that, Lucy. Seagrave intended it as a parody on Constable. Actually, if you look closely you'll see the trees are in a slightly different place. But you must agree it displays a droll sense of humour.

Soapy If you don't like that, I've got two kittens playing with a ball of wool.

Victor (*quickly*) Why don't you set your easel up in the conservatory, Seagrave? The light's better in there.

Soapy Right.

Soapy gathers up his easel with difficulty and weaves his way into the conservatory

Kevin enters looking rather self-conscious in a velvet smoking jacket

Lucy You look very smart, Kevin.

Kevin (*proudly*) I'm having my picture painted.

Lucy So I've heard.

Soapy returns for his paints

Kevin Will I do like this?

Soapy studies him closely

Soapy Are you always that colour?

Kevin Well, yes.

Soapy I'll need more purple. (*He begins mixing paints*)

Kevin What sort of pose would you like me to adopt?

Soapy Arms folded. Then I won't have to paint your hands.

Kevin (*folding his arms*) Like this?

Soapy looks closer

Soapy Stand still for a minute.

Kevin I am standing still.

Soapy Well, one of us is moving …(*He stares*) Is one of your ears bigger than the other?

Kevin I don't think so …

Soapy It looks bigger. If it looks bigger on the painting, don't blame me.

Victor Perhaps if you painted him in profile …
Soapy But then there's the nose.
Victor I see what you mean.
Soapy You'd better go through there and stand amongst the ferns. I'll
see what I can do.

Kevin exits into the conservatory

It's not going to be easy.

Soapy follows Kevin

Lucy Are you sure he's a famous painter, Victor?
Victor Yes. Why?
Lucy He seems very strange.
Victor That's because he's a genius.
Lucy And he's drunk.
Victor That's how you can tell the professional — they're usually
drunk. A professional drinks instead of painting — the amateur paints
instead of drinking.
Lucy I didn't know that.

Soapy returns

Soapy A little libation before I commence. (*He drinks the cleaning
fluid. Shaking his head*) My God! That's got a kick.

Soapy staggers back into the conservatory

Lucy (*drily*) He's certainly very professional …

Lucy exits

Victor takes the whisky bottle and hides it away in the cabinet

Valerie enters looking worried

Valerie Victor, the bank manager's come back — and he has someone
with him.
Victor I wonder who that can be?
Valerie You haven't been up to anything, have you?
Victor Certainly not. You'd better send them in.

Victor closes the doors to the conservatory

Tank Turner enters the room. He is followed by Toby, who is a few years younger but similar in bulk and severity

Valerie stands anxiously in the rear

Tank Hello, Bodger.
Valerie (*blankly*) Bodger?
Victor Perhaps you'd make some tea, Val.
Valerie Yes. Where's Kevin?
Victor Having his picture painted.
Valerie His picture? Why?
Victor For posterity.
Valerie Oh.

Valerie exits in bewilderment

Tank Bodger, I'd like you to meet Toby. Toby — Bodger Blake — must have been at Benthams in your time.

They shake hands. Toby regards Victor thoughtfully

Toby Bodger ... (*Frowning*) I don't seem to remember you ...
Victor I've changed a great deal since then. I was all freckles and ink-blots in those days.
Toby Bodger ... I don't recall the name. Bodger ...
Victor I was sometimes known as Smudge.
Toby Smudge ... (*Shaking his head*) No ...
Victor I was only at Benthams for a short time. Before I went up to Oxford.
Tank Where he got his blue, Toby.
Victor Against the All Blacks.
Tank I thought it was the Springboks.
Victor That was the next season.
Toby Sorry, I still don't remember you.
Tank He remembers Pop Askew, don't you, Bodger?
Victor Yes — Old Pop.
Tank There was a character.
Victor One of the best.
Toby Personally I found him vicious.
Victor Vicious but fair, Toby.
Tank He once gave me six of the best for cutting net practice.

Victor That was old Pop for you — couldn't stand slackers.
Toby That was nothing. The old swine took a rope's end to me for smoking behind the pavilion.
Victor I don't know what you're complaining about, Toby — he once laid me out with a cricket stump for climbing the ivy on the west wall.
Tank Good Lord.
Toby I don't remember any ivy on the west wall.
Victor You wouldn't. I pulled most of it down when he hit me. Still, it made a man of me. And Pop and I have become great friends.
Toby Oh? I understood the sadistic old brute died last year.
Victor (*shocked*) What, dead? Old Pop. I thought he was indestructible. We shan't see his like again. (*Emotionally*) Excuse me, gentlemen — I must compose myself ...

Victor turns away but finds he is followed by the suspicious Toby

Toby And what do you think of the team this year ... Bodger?
Victor The team?
Toby The Old Boys?
Victor What do I think of them? Not enough weight in the scrum, Toby. They're weak in the loose — and they're not getting enough ball in the line-out. They won't do any good until they get more possession.
Toby But they haven't lost a match in two seasons.
Victor That's no reason for complacency. It's coming — mark my words — all the signs are there. They're not training hard enough — they've had it too easy. They should have played against the All Blacks with a busted shoulder.
Tank I thought you said ——
Victor Ever faced the Haka, Toby?
Toby No.
Victor Well, I have — and it's a chilling prospect. They come at you like this ... led by an All Black of Maori descent ... (*He begins to give a passable imitation of the Haka. He bows his legs and stands flat-footed. He crosses his clenched fist. He begins to beat his thighs. He bangs his thighs, chest and head with his fists. He advances menacing and crablike and pointing at the ground*)

Tank and Toby move back

(*Chanting*)
                        Ka mate! Ka mate!
                        Ka ora! Ka ora!

Tenei te Tangata puhuru huru
Nana nei i tiki mai'
(*He continues to advance*)
'Whakawhiti te ra
A upane ka upane
Upane, Kaupane
Whiti te ra! Hi!'
(*He leaps into the air*)

Toby and Tank fall back further

Tank That must have been very intimidating.

Victor It is — but you mustn't give ground. That's given me a thirst. Should we have something stronger whilst we're waiting for the tea?

Toby No, I need to keep a clear head.

Tank Toby's here on business.

Victor (*cautiously*) Business?

Tank You see, Bodger — after I left yesterday, I couldn't help thinking about those diamonds. And I wondered if I'd been too hasty.

Victor Ah. I thought so. The flushed cheek — the bright eye. You've got diamond fever, Tank. I saw that in Mad Henry — those wild eyes glaring in their sockets ——

Toby Yes. Quite. Perhaps we could see these diamonds?

Victor Certainly. (*He takes out the pouch and spreads the diamonds on the desk*)

Tank Toby here's an expert.

Victor What?

Toby Not an expert exactly. I keep the jewellers in the Market Place.

Victor (*weakly*) Rogers' — in the Market Place?

Toby That's right.

They study the diamonds

Tank They seem to be smaller.

Victor No, the diamonds haven't got smaller — your eyes have got bigger. That's what diamonds can do to a man. I've seen men sell their souls for a handful of these beauties — even kill for them.

Tank What do you think, Toby?

Toby Well, I don't know much about uncut diamonds — but they're supposed to be cold on the tongue ... (*He licks the crystal*) This is bitter.

Victor Of course it tastes bitter. I had to get them out of the country. They were smuggled north in a camel's rectum.

Toby Oh. Perhaps I will have that drink …

Victor Let's drink to success, gentlemen. All right. It's a gamble. We're all gambling on Mad Henry. Perhaps we'll never find the diamonds — but it's a risk worth taking … If you'll just make your cheques out to ——

Toby If you don't mind, I'll like to think about it a little longer.

Tank Toby's understandably cautious. He got his fingers burnt rather badly a few years ago — following my advice, I'm afraid.

Toby I don't blame you, Tank — but if I ever come across the swine responsible …

Victor The world's full of them, Toby. Who were they?

Toby Rockfast Investments. Ever heard of them?

Victor, who is about to pour, puts down the decanter

Victor Sounds familiar …

Tank Toby's still very bitter.

Toby Turned out to be a bunch of crooks. I lost the lot. The only consolation was that they sent the ringleader away for a few years.

Tank He must be out by now.

Victor Well, I suppose it's no good letting it eat away at you. Poor devil's paid for what he did.

Toby He hasn't paid enough. If we were to meet him now, what would we do, Tank?

Tank Debag the blighter. The Bentham way.

Victor Hear, hear! But would you know him again?

Toby No, I couldn't bear to attend the trial.

Tank We only saw press photographs of him leaving the court.

Toby Always had a coat over his head.

Tank I remember his shoes.

Toby Yes … always wore two-toned shoes …

Tank Suede. Typical rotter.

They stare down at Victor's shoes which are suede. There is an embarrassed silence

No offence, Bodger.

Victor (*smiling smoothly*) None taken, Toby. (*He starts to pour*)

Toby No, don't bother. I must get back to the shop — I've rather neglected it this week …

The rattle of tea cups precedes Lucy entering with the tea tray

Victor Wait — here's the tea. At least have some tea.

Lucy Val said you'd like some tea.

Victor sees with alarm that she's wearing the bracelet

Victor (*hastily*) Thank you, Lucy.

He seizes her wrist, obscuring the bracelet, and kisses her cheek. She looks surprised. They put the tray down together. He stills holds on to her wrist

   Tank, you've met Lucy?
Tank Yes, she showed me that lovely ——
Victor And this is Toby. He's a friend of Tank's ...
Toby Hello.

Toby shakes Lucy's hand and finds he's pumping Victor's arm as well. They stare at Victor

Victor (*beaming*) We're inseparable these days. Almost joined at the
   hip.
Lucy Perhaps you'd like to pour the tea, Victor.
Victor Of course.

Victor escorts a puzzled Lucy to the door

   Hurry back.

Lucy exits

   I miss her as soon as she's gone. I think the world of her.
Tank I know. Bodger's bought her this ——
Victor Milk, Tank, sugar?
Tank Both. You'll be interested in this, Toby. Bodger's bought her this
   magnificent ——
Victor What about you, Toby?
Toby Just milk.
Tank — a really superb piece ——

Soapy emerges wearily from the conservatory

Victor (*desperately*) Have you met Seagrave Simpson — the artist —
   member of the Royal Academy?
Soapy And painter to Her Majesty.

Toby and Tank look impressed

Toby Really? Her Majesty?
Tank I say.
Toby What are you doing here?
Soapy Going for a leak.
Victor (*hastily*) Seagrave's painting my brother-in-law, Kevin.
Tank Kevin...?
Victor Bunce.
Tank Yes, can never remember the fellow's name. He's been put up for the Rotary, Toby.
Toby Really?
Tank Estate agent.
Toby I suppose we have to have one.
Victor How's the painting going, Seagrave?
Soapy Not an easy subject. Keeps moving — scratching his nose — and generally farting about.
Victor Across the hall, Seagrave.
Soapy Right.

Soapy exits into the hall

Kevin appears from the conservatory looking rather grand

Kevin (*loftily*) Oh, I'm sorry I wasn't here to greet you, gentlemen, but as you see I'm having my portrait painted by Seagrave Simpson.
Tank That must cost a great deal.
Kevin It's worth it — and we don't talk money where art's concerned, do we? Have you had yours done?
Tank Well, no.
Kevin You do surprise me.
Toby How did you get in touch with him?
Kevin I didn't. He approached me.
Toby Why?
Kevin Why? Saw something in my face — character, I think...

They all study Kevin's face in surprise

Valerie enters

Valerie Kevin, there's a man in the hall says he's painting you.
Kevin (*proudly*) That's right.
Valerie Why?

Kevin Why? Why does everyone ask that? Because I have an interesting face — that's why. He should know — he's an artist. Ask him.

Valerie I will ...

Valerie exits

Kevin She doesn't see it. Too close. Hasn't noticed the changes. What life's done to me. How my character's been formed. Takes an artist to see that. Well, excuse me — I must get back to my pose whilst it's fresh in my mind ...

Kevin exits into conservatory

Toby Well, I must say it's come to something when an estate agent's having his picture painted.

Tank Bit of an ego trip, if you ask me.

Victor Seagrave may be able to squeeze you in tomorrow.

Toby (*brightening*) Do you think so?

Victor Could be arranged.

Tank But would he want to?

Victor I saw the way he was looking at you. He was weighing you up.

Toby Really?

Victor He saw something you only see at the bottom of a scrum. Grit and determination. He saw two of the finest men who ever punted leather. You could hang it in the clubhouse.

Toby That's a thought.

Tank Perhaps you'd keep us informed, Bodger?

Victor Of course.

Victor is escorting them to the hall

Toby Bodger, would you mind showing us again?

Victor (*cautiously*) The diamonds?

Toby No, the Haka. I thought Tank and I might do it at the club dinner.

Victor (*smiling*) Follow me, gentlemen ...

He commences the Haka. They watch and then join in

Lucy enters with a plate of biscuits

They pass Lucy and they conclude the Haka with a leap in the air and exit

Lucy puts down the plate

Victor returns

Lucy What was that all about?
Victor Just an old Maori custom. (*He takes a biscuit*)
Lucy Victor, Seagrave Simpson ...
Victor Yes?
Lucy He is a reputable painter?
Victor Of course. Just a little eccentric.
Lucy But he is well regarded?
Victor In the highest circles. Why?
Lucy He wants to paint me.
Victor Splendid. It's quite a privilege, Lucy.
Lucy He says he's seen something he'd like to get down on the canvas ...
Victor I know the feeling.
Lucy So you think I should have it done?
Victor Of course. It's a wonderful opportunity.
Lucy Then I will.
Victor Good.
Lucy He wants to paint me in ... the ...
Victor The conservatory?
Lucy No — the nude ...

Lucy exits smiling

Victor's biscuit stops a few inches from his lips

Victor What?

CURTAIN

SCENE 2

The same. The following afternoon

As the CURTAIN *rises, Victor is on the phone*

Victor I'm sure he can squeeze you in, Tank — probably later today.
(*Darkly*) There may be a cancellation. ... Yes. (*He breaks off*)

Soapy enters from the conservatory proudly bearing a canvas

(*Into the* phone) I have to go now. Excuse me. Bye ... (*He replaces the phone*)

Soapy Ready for it?

Victor nods. Soapy proudly reveals the canvas. It is a lurid portrait in vivid purples and greens. Victor stares in astonishment

Victor Who is it? No, let me rephrase that. What is it?

Soapy (*indignantly*) It's Kevin.

Victor It's nothing like Kevin. I've never seen him that colour, even when he's angry.

Soapy That's my style. Bold use of colour and broad brush strokes. It's not a photograph. I've brought out the inner man — the one he hides from the world.

Victor Well, now I can see why he's hiding it! It's terrible.

Soapy That's how I see him. You wouldn't understand — you're not an artist.

Victor Neither are you.

Soapy He's going to love this picture — trust me. Notice how the eyes follow you around the room?

Victor Yes, I must say, that's like Kevin.

Soapy You see, it's growing on you. That's the usual reaction to my portraits. First revulsion, then fascination, and finally, enchantment.

Victor I hope you're right because I've been lining up a few commissions. By the way, I understand you intend to paint Lucy in the nude?

Soapy No, I shall remain fully clothed. I just hope I can keep my brush steady.

Victor I forbid it.

Soapy Why? Don't you want me to capture the essential woman — her sensuality, her luminosity?

Victor No — I haven't seen it myself yet.

Soapy I thought you were engaged?

Victor We are — unofficially.

Soapy And you've never seen her naked?

Victor No.

Soapy Not even — unofficially?

Victor No! She's only just out of mourning — it would be unseemly.

Soapy Never mind. (*Confidentially*) I'll tell you what she's like ...

Victor I don't want you to tell me what she's like! Take care, Soapy, or I might tell her what you're like.

Soapy But you won't, will you? Because you can't tell her what I'm like without telling her what you're like ... And you won't do that, will you?

Victor Why not?

Soapy Because you'll spoil a perfect set-up. Rich widow — ready to marry you and solve all your financial problems. You wouldn't risk that. No, I shall paint her in the nude — and I just hope I shall rise to the occasion.

There are sounds off of the front door opening

Sounds as if Kevin's back.

Victor Take that daub into the conservatory. I have to prepare him.

Soapy crosses to the conservatory

Soapy Don't spoil the surprise.

Victor Don't you mean shock?

Soapy exits with the picture

Victor pours a drink

Kevin enters excitedly

Kevin Well, have you seen it?

Victor Yes.

He offers Kevin a drink

Kevin No, it's too early for me. Is it in there?

Victor One moment, Kevin. First of all, it's not a photograph.

Kevin I realize that.

Victor It may surprise you, because we can never see ourselves as others see us. Think of the total surprise we feel when we see ourselves on a security camera.

Kevin I don't.

Victor Don't you?

Kevin I know what I look like.

Victor You mean you think you know what you look like.

Kevin I only have to look in the mirror.

Victor That's a reflection. It's not the same.

Kevin Isn't it?

Victor When you look in the mirror you can't read what it says on your T-shirt, can you?

Kevin Well, no.

Victor There you are then. You go in there expecting to see a reflection and you're going to be disappointed.

Kevin Now I'm intrigued. I must see it ...

Kevin exits into the conservatory

Victor takes a deep drink and listens. There is a long, loud hollow groan from the conservatory. Victor finishes his drink and pours another

Kevin returns carrying the portrait. His face is set. He throws it to the ground and jumps on it. He smashes it. He kicks it. He breaks it into pieces and thrusts the pieces into the waste bin

Victor watches him in silence

Victor (*after a pause*) You don't like it.

Kevin Why? Why do I always fall for it? Why do I believe your stories? When am I going to learn? This was just another scheme to make money. He's not an artist — and his name's not Seagrave Simpson, is it?

Victor No. (*He hesitates*) I met him inside. He was known as Soapy.

Kevin Soapy!

Victor Soapy Simpson, due to his habit of dressing his hair with liquid soap. When it got wet he came out in bubbles. So we called him Soapy.

Kevin stares at him for a moment and begins to smile. He chuckles

Victor (*looking relieved*) What's this? My brother-in-law's smiling again. This is more like it. You're seeing the funny side.

Kevin No — I'm smiling because that seedy, lecherous rogue out there is going to see your girlfriend in the buff, and there's nothing you can do about it. You'll just have to grin and bear it — or rather she'll have to bare it!

Victor (*frowning*) That's enough, Kevin. I'm not enjoying the prospect.

Kevin No, but I'm sure he will!

Victor He's painting her — that's all.

Lucy enters in a robe

Lucy Is Seagrave ready for me?

Kevin (*smirking*) Oh, yes — more than ready. (*He crosses to get a drink, stifling laughter*)

Victor (*taking Lucy to one side*) Lucy, do you have to do this?
Lucy Why? There's nothing wrong, is there?
Victor No — but in the nude ...
Lucy He wants to bring out the sensual side of my nature.
Victor You can't show him the sensual side of your nature — you
haven't shown it to me yet.

Victor observes Kevin's shaking shoulders

Lucy But, Victor — we're talking art not sex. Evil is in the eye of the
beholder.
Victor That's what worries me.
Lucy Seagrave wants to cut through convention and get down to the
bare essentials. After all, the human body is nothing to be ashamed
of ...
Victor Well, no but ——
Lucy I'm certainly not ashamed of mine.
Victor (*hissing*) Then why haven't I seen it?
Lucy You will — when it's exhibited.
Victor Exhibited! The woman I love on show — to be leered at by
strangers — wearing absolutely nothing.
Lucy I shall be wearing something, silly.
Victor You will? You had me worried for a moment. What are you
wearing?
Lucy My bracelet ...

Lucy exits into the conservatory

Kevin (*choking*) That's not going to hide much.

Valerie enters. She is also wearing a robe

Victor smiles

Victor Kevin ...

Kevin turns and his giggles die away

Kevin Valerie! You're not going in there?
Valerie Yes. He wants me in the background.
Kevin How far in the background.
Valerie Not very far.
Kevin With nothing on.

Valerie No — I shall be wearing my pearls.

Kevin Is that all?

Valerie Yes. He wants us to wear our jewellery. He says it'll be a talking point.

Kevin There'll be plenty to talk about without the pearls.

Valerie What do you mean?

Kevin Nothing.

Valerie He's going to call it "Reclining Nudes — with jewellery".

Kevin Not reclining please! What about "Nudes Amongst Ferns"? Or "Nudes Behind Gauze"? Leave something for the imagination, for God's sake.

Valerie What's the matter, Kevin? Are you ashamed of my body?

Kevin No.

Valerie You didn't object to Lucy being painted in the nude. Perhaps you think she has a better figure?

Kevin No, but you're my wife.

Valerie Are you sure that's the reason? Or is that why you always make love with the lights out?

Kevin Valerie, please — lower your voice.

Valerie Well, I'm proud of my body, even if you're not. And I can't help recalling that when I went topless in Ibiza, you threw a towel over me!

Valerie marches into the conservatory

Kevin puts down his drink and starts to follow. Victor stops him

Victor Where are you going?

Kevin I'm going to stop this.

Victor You can't. You'll give the game away.

Kevin I don't care.

Victor Kevin, you haven't asked me why Soapy was in prison …

Kevin Why?

Victor He's a jewel thief.

Kevin What?

Victor And a leopard doesn't change his spots …

Kevin You mean?

Victor Why the insistence that the ladies wear their jewellery? It's delightful in its simplicity. He's painting — they're starkers. He'll remove that bracelet under some pretext and promptly leg it. They won't be able to chase him because they'll be naked.

Kevin Then shouldn't we stop him?

Victor No.

Kevin But what about the pearls?

Victor We all know they're paste, Kevin. It's the bracelet he's after. I've seen the way he's been looking at it. And it'll be the solution to all our problems. Lucy won't return the bracelet to me — so I can't return it to the shop. And I certainly can't afford to buy it. But if it were stolen I won't have to ...

Kevin Then who will?

Victor Not me — it's on approval. It's not my property. I suppose they'll have some sort of insurance ...

Kevin No, I won't go through with it — it's illegal.

Victor Kevin, did you recognize the man who was with Turner yesterday?

Kevin No, but he looked familiar.

Victor Yes. That was Rogers — the jeweller.

Kevin My God! He hadn't come for the bracelet?

Victor No, but he will do — anytime now.

Kevin But he's chief Rotarian!

Victor And your name will be mud ... (*His voice dies away*)

Tank and Toby enter from the hall looking deadly serious

Tank Sorry to burst in like this, Bodger. But this couldn't wait.

Victor But you're too early. Seagrave has another sitting.

Toby We haven't come to sit. When I left yesterday I took one of your diamonds with me. I thought I'd run a few tests before I invested my money. You may be interested to know that when I immersed it in liquid it disappeared.

A low groan from Kevin

Victor Disappeared!

Toby It turned out to be some kind of lavatory cleaner.

Victor My God! You know what this means? Mad Henry was mad after all. Full marks, Toby. You've saved us a great deal of money.

Toby Whilst I was talking diamonds with Tank here, he mentioned a bracelet you'd given to your fiancée. It sounded familiar. I subsequently found that it had been taken from my shop on approval. Since the money is still outstanding I'd like its return. And don't bother to make out a cheque. Tank's advised me against it.

Lucy enters from the conservatory followed by Valerie

Ah. Here's the lady in question.

Victor (*hurriedly*) The lady hasn't time for this. She's sitting for her portrait.

Lucy But I'm not.

Victor What?

Lucy Seagrave's run off through the gardens.

Victor I knew it! The man was bogus! We've been deceived. He wormed his way into our confidence only to betray us. He's a thief! (*He snatches up Lucy's wrist*) See, the bracelet's gone. He took advantage of your state of undress, Lucy, and bolted with it

Lucy No he didn't, Victor. It's on the other wrist. (*She shows him the bracelet*)

Victor What? Then why did he run?

Lucy (*smiling*) I think we'd better make a clean breast of it, Val.

Valerie If you'll excuse the expression …

They turn together upstage and shimmy like a couple of strippers and throw open their robes. Kevin and Victor give a concerted groan. The ladies turn to reveal that they are fully dressed

Lucy We thought there was something dodgy about Seagrave.

Valerie Especially when we discovered that he'd slept in the back of a three-wheel van last night.

Lucy We did this to teach you both a lesson.

Victor But why did he run?

Lucy I told him I thought the police had arrived.

Victor What?

Toby Well, I'm afraid you're still going to lose that bracelet, Mrs Myers — unless you're prepared to pay for it...

Lucy Pay for it? I'm afraid I can't. You see I haven't got any money.

Victor No money?

Lucy And my house is heavily mortgaged. You see my husband was rather rash with the family money. He put most of it into Rockfast Investments — and we all know what happened there.

All (*indignantly*) Rockfast Investments!

Victor (*belatedly*) Rockfast Investments!

Lucy But don't worry. (*She lays the bracelet on the desk*) I never wanted the bracelet. You can have it.

Victor But then why did you keep it?

Lucy To see you squirm.

Victor Squirm?

Lucy Like you did in the box — at the Old Bailey. I attended every day of the trial — that was why I recognized you at once.

Victor But you didn't say anything.

Lucy No I thought it would be fun to spend your money for a change
— instead of you spending mine. Unfortunately, you don't appear to
have any.

Toby You mean he's Rockfast Investments?

Tank Look at the shoes, Toby.

Toby Yes … suede.

Tank The footwear of a rotter.

Toby and Tank advance on Victor

Victor It wasn't me — it was my accountant — he had a wife and
six ——

Tank Ever faced the Haka, Bodger?

Victor What?

Toby and Tank advance on Victor performing the Haka and chanting

Victor turns and flees into the hall. Tank and Toby pursue him

There are sounds of doors slamming

*Val and Lucy cross to the downstage window and crane their necks to
view the road. Kevin follows*

Valerie Look at Victor!

Lucy I didn't know he could run so fast.

Kevin They're running faster.

Valerie They've caught him by the bus stop.

Kevin I think he's trying to join the queue.

Valerie Everyone's staring.

Lucy What are they doing to him?

Kevin I think it's what's known as debagging — the Bentham way.

Valerie What will the neighbours say?

Kevin laughs

Kevin (*returning to his desk*) This calls for a celebration.

Valerie What are you doing?

Kevin Making out a cheque. If Lucy doesn't want the bracelet you may
as well have it.

Valerie But it's so expensive.

Kevin But it's genuine, Val. The vase is a copy, the fireplace is fake,
there's a simulated log effect burning in the hearth — it's time we had
something genuine around here.

Valerie Oh, Kevin. (*She kisses him*) You're genuine — that's all that matters. (*She picks up the bracelet*) I wonder what it'll look like with my blue dress?

Valerie exits excitedly

Lucy I think you've made a very good investment there, Kevin. (*She turns from the window*) They're back.

Tank and Toby enter. Toby is neatly folding a pair of trousers

Toby I think we'll hang these in the clubhouse, Tank.
Tank Good idea.
Toby Just one final detail. The bracelet, Mrs Myers.
Kevin That won't be necessary. I've bought it for my wife. (*He hands the cheque to Toby*)

Toby glances at Tank who nods

Toby Yes, that seems satisfactory. Thank you ... er, Kevin, isn't it?
Kevin Yes.
Toby Hope to see you at the Rotary sometime ...

Toby and Tank make for the door

Tank After all, one can't choose one's relatives ...

Toby and Tank exit

There is the sound of the front door closing

Lucy I wonder what's happened to Victor?
Kevin Probably hiding in the laurels.
Lucy The neighbours must be enjoying the prospect. (*Smiling*) I hope he's wearing clean underwear.
Kevin If he is — it's mine.

Urgent ringing of the front doorbell. Kevin and Lucy smile at each other

Lucy Was that the front door?
Kevin I didn't hear anything.

Loud knocking

Did you hear that?
Lucy What?
Kevin Knocking.
Lucy No.

There is the sound of running footsteps

Another urgent ringing of the back doorbell

Kevin Was that the back door?
Lucy I don't think so ...

A crash from the conservatory

   Victor enters in his shirt tails looking pink and uncomfortable

Lucy regards him silently for a moment

Lucy Victor, when you got up this morning ... did you forget something?
Victor Lucy, I ——
Lucy I think I'll see if that bracelet goes with the blue dress. (*She begins to cross*)
Victor I don't suppose you'll speak to me again.
Lucy Oh, I don't know, Victor.

She turns and kisses him lightly on the lips

Nice legs ...

   Lucy exits

Victor Kevin.
Kevin What?
Victor Did you see that kiss?
Kevin She hasn't any money.
Victor What's that got to do with luminosity?
Kevin You don't stand a chance.
Victor Why not?
Kevin Victor, you've had all her money — you're out of prison — you're out of work — and you're out of your trousers.

Victor (*considering*) Yes ... but apart from that.

Kevin gives a loud internal groan

Curtain

FURNITURE AND PROPERTY LIST

ACT I
SCENE 1

On stage: Chintz-covered suite
Fireplace. *In it*: simulated log fire. *On mantelpiece*: vase
Leather-topped desk. *In drawer*: cheque book. *On it*: manuscript,
phone, notepad and pen. *Beside it*: waste bin
High-backed swivel chair
French doors open
Revolving cocktail cabinet. *In it*: glasses, decanter of scotch, bottle
of malt whisky, various other bottles. *On it*: silver cigarette box
Ferns and flowers in conservatory area

Off stage: Briefcase (**Kevin**)
Walking stick (**Victor**)

ACT I
SCENE 2

Strike: Glasses

Re-set: Walking stick leaning by desk

Off stage: Coat (**Kevin**)

Personal: **Victor**: jewel box containing diamond bracelet; wallet containing credit cards and cheque book; crumpled piece of paper in
pocket; crystals in a pouch hung around his neck
Tank: cheque book

ACT II
SCENE 1

Check: French doors open

Off stage: Canvas (**Soapy**)
Easel, canvas, paints, brushes, mixing jar, palette, jar of cleaning
fluid, rag (**Soapy**)

        Tray containing, cups and saucers, pot of tea, jug of milk (**Lucy**)
        Plate of biscuits (**Lucy**)

Personal: **Soapy**: battered five-pound note in pocket

ACT II
SCENE 2

Off stage: Lurid canvas portrait in vivid purples and greens (**Soapy**)
        Lurid portrait in vivid purples and greens (for wrecking) (**Kevin**)
        Pair of trousers (**Toby**)

LIGHTING PLOT

Property fittings required: nil

ACT I, Scene 1

To open: General interior lighting with daylight in conservatory

No cues

ACT I, Scene 2

To open: General interior lighting with daylight in conservatory

No cues

ACT II, Scene 1

To open: General interior lighting with daylight in conservatory

No cues

ACT II, Scene 2

To open: General interior lighting with daylight in conservatory

No cues

EFFECTS PLOT

ACT I

Cue 1   **Kevin**: "That won't be necessary."   (Page 13)
Phone on desk rings

ACT II

Cue 2   **Soapy**: " … I shall rise to the occasion."   (Page 50)
Sound of front door opening

Cue 3   **Victor** flees. **Toby** and **Tank** pursue him   (Page 56)
Doors slamming

Cue 4   **Toby** and **Tank** exit   (Page 57)
Front door closes

Cue 5   **Kevin**: "If he is — it's mine."   (Page 57)
Urgent ringing of front doorbell

Cue 6   **Kevin**: "I didn't hear anything."   (Page 57)
Loud knocking

Cue 7   **Lucy**: "No."   (Page 58)
Running footsteps followed by urgent ringing of back doorbell

Cue 8   **Lucy**: "I don't think so ..."   (Page 58)
Crash from conservatory

Lightning Source UK Ltd.
Milton Keynes UK
UKOW06f1235140916

282963UK00015B/250/P